RAILWAY NOSTALGIA AROUND WARWICKSHIRE

Front endpaper (left)
The view from the fireman's seat of preserved Ivatt No. 46521 on the Gloucestershire Warwickshire Railway line in April 1993. *(The author)*

Front endpaper (right)
Ex-LMS Fowler class 4F 0-6-0 No. 44187 with a goods train approaching Alcester from Broom junction on 27 August 1961. *(Ray Green)*

Title page
Flecknoe station.

Rear endpaper (left)
The sidings, at the foot of the incline, of what was the Edge Hill Light Railway on 14 July 1942, and No. 2 0-6-0 tank stands derelict with decaying brake van and tipping wagons. *(National Railway Museum)*

Rear endpaper (right)
Electrification work on the Coventry to Birmingham line at Berkswell station in December 1965. *(Coventry Evening Telegraph)*

Frontispiece. LMS 'Jubilee' 4-6-0 No. 45576 BOMBAY stands with a passenger train to Derby and North Midlands alongside platform 7 at Birmingham New Street station on 14 July 1962. A truly impressive picture showing the magnificent curve of the station roof and the decorative stonework. *(Ray Reed)*

RAILWAY NOSTALGIA AROUND WARWICKSHIRE

Compiled by D. Hibbs

W.D. WHARTON
Wellingborough

First published in 1993 by
W.D. Wharton
37 Sheep Street
Wellingborough
Northamptonshire NN8 1BX

ISBN 0 9518557 4 3

Designed and typeset by John Hardaker, Wollaston, Northamptonshire
Printed and bound in Great Britain by
Woolnough Bookbinding Ltd
Irthlingborough, Northamptonshire

CONTENTS

DEDICATION

To my parents
Horace and Edith Hibbs

ACKNOWLEDGEMENTS

Compiling this book would have been an impossible task without the help and encouragement of many Warwickshire train enthusiasts.

I must thank Pat Walker for giving me information on his own engine, 'Byfield 2', for lending me loads of books and other information, and getting me a ride on the footplate of Ivatt No. 46521, and for putting me in touch with Dick Blenkinsop; Iain Pardoe; Malcolm Walker and the Gloucestershire Warwickshire Railway at Toddington. Also, Graham Stokes for all his information on the railway network in Warwickshire and for showing me around; Bob Darvill for his section on industrial locomotives; Ralph Ward, Ray Green, Ray Reed, John Cain, Martyn S. Lane, Peter Thomas, Duggy Hargrave, Derek Smith, Steve Standbridge and Wayne Finch for the use of their photographs; and Paul Hayting of Rugby for photographic printing. Thanks, too, to the *Coventry Evening Telegraph* for giving me access to their archives and permitting me to reproduce a selection from their photographic library. I acknowlege the help of the National Railway Museum, the source of many unique pictures in this book, and I am grateful to Nuneaton Railway Society and Stratford-upon-Avon Railway Society for allowing me to attend their meetings. Also, I thank my family for their tolerance, and most of all Robert Wharton for his support and enthusiasm, and John Hardaker for his expertise in editing and putting the book together.

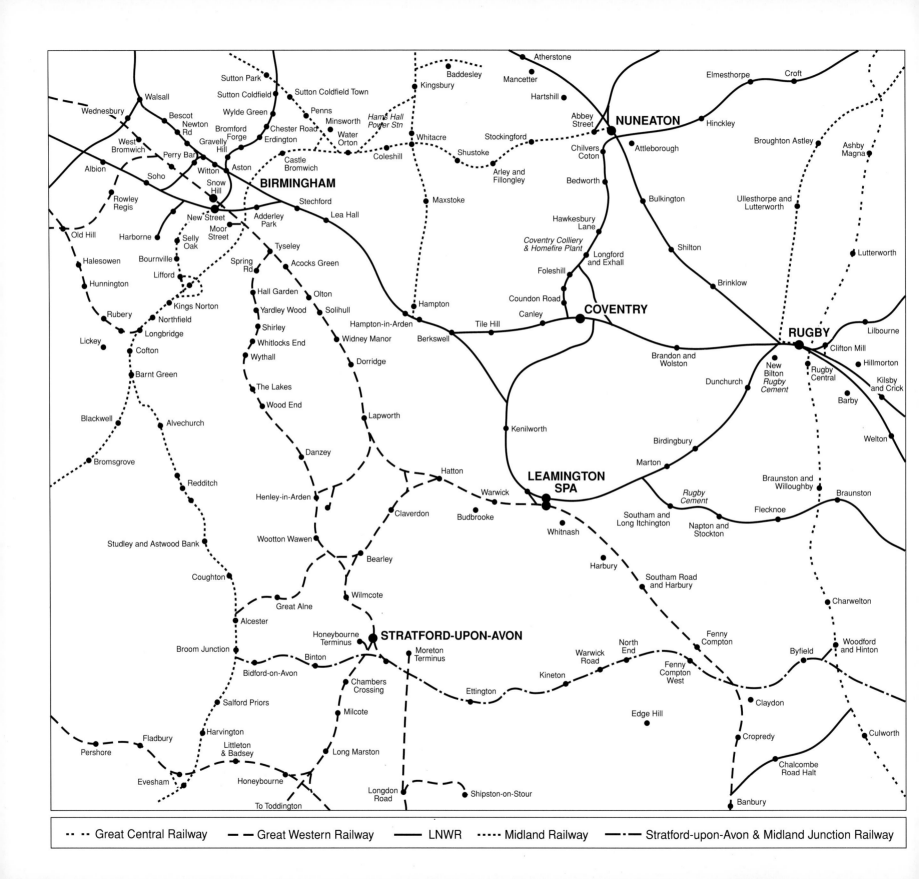

Great Central Railway ----- | Great Western Railway - - - | LNWR ——— | Midland Railway ········· | Stratford-upon-Avon & Midland Junction Railway —·—·—

INTRODUCTION

In *Railway Nostalgia Around Warwickshire* I have tried to portray the development and decline of the railways in the county.

My first taste of trains was in Gloucestershire during the Second World War. I learned to tell the time because of the punctuality of the trains half a mile away on the Gloucester to Stroud line. This was followed by travelling to school from Cashes Green to Stroud on the long-gone rail car.

In the 50s I was to spend five years at school in Somerset catching the train from Birmingham New Street, changing at Bristol Temple Meads and on to Weston-Super-Mare. For half-term breaks I had to catch the slow train back to Stonehouse (Gloucestershire). As was the way in those days I was put in the guard's charge until it was felt I was old enough to look after myself.

I finished my education at Birmingham Photographic College (part of the Arts School) spending two years travelling from Coventry to Birmingham New Street every day, hoping to catch the 7.50 a.m. slow train in and the fast train home in the afternoon.

Now a lot older and a little wiser, I am the owner of the land that used to be Flecknoe station (Weedon to Leamington line). Sadly the buildings were removed and sold to Stockton Cricket Club, but all the old fencing remains, as do the stanchions which the goods building used to stand on.

After the First World War a Mr Twigger was Station Master. He had two porters to assist him – one who worked in the mornings until 2 p.m. and the other who worked from 2 to 10 p.m. They must all have lived in the row of four red-brick terraced station cottages that still stand, the largest being called Station House. When the line was closed Mr Harry Adkins was the Station Master. He combined his job with being Licensee of *The Old Olive Bush* one mile away in Flecknoe village.

It is a great pity that small lines and small trains were not recorded in greater depth. They really were the bread-and-butter of the great days of steam. I know of two farmers whose parents moved to local farms from Wales. They milked the cows in the morning, walked all the livestock to the nearest railway, loaded up and arrived at Flecknoe and Frankton stations, respectively, in time to walk the cows to their new farm and do the evening milking. Meanwhile, all their household and farm possessions were being unloaded from the goods train sidings, but nobody thought enough of the event to record it on film.

Maybe this book will jog a few memories, and result in the discovering of some long-forgotten photographs. I certainly hope so.

D. Hibbs
Flecknoe

COVENTRY
and around

1. Coventry City station showing the extensions made in 1901-3. Boys in Eton collars and young ladies in boots watch the photographer. Behind the tram is a horse-drawn 'Brougham'. The gateway on the right is the entrance to the Railway Hotel, now The Rocket. *(Coventry City Library)*

2. Coventry station forecourt just after the end of the Second World War. *(Ray Green)*

3. Coventry station in April 1985. *(Coventry Evening Telegraph)*

4. An aerial view of Coventry City station and goods yard looking east, taken in 1919. The large factory (top left) is the present Rolls Royce site. Like all stations up to the 1950s that had goods yards, horses were used to transport goods to local destinations. A number of horse-drawn wagons can be seen in this picture. The bridge in the foreground is the Spencer Road bridge, and behind that is the Coventry-Kenilworth road bridge. There is a passenger train (top right) heading off on the Kenilworth-Leamington Spa line. The main line heads for London.

(Coventry City Library)

5. A March 1990 view, looking west over where the goods yard used to be (see opposite picture). Spencer bridge remains intact. The line to the left goes to Canley Halt and on to Birmingham New Street, while that to the right heads for Nuneaton. The multi-storey car park built with the new station had proved inadequate to meet the growing needs, hence the old goods yard area being used as an overflow car park, which itself looks close to saturation point. The Rocket public house in the foreground used to be the Railway Hotel. *(Coventry Evening Telegraph)*

6. Coventry station in 1879 with a waiting 'up' passenger train and a goods train alongside. The loco on the right, which is taking on water, is an LNWR 'Large Bloomer' which was designed for the Southern Region in 1851 by McConnell.
The engine in front of the goods train is a DX Class 0-6-0. *(Coventry City Library)*

7. Part of the embankment carrying the Coventry loop line at Pinley in 1914. *(Coventry City Library)*

8. The platforms of Coventry station on a wet night in November 1966. The Station Tower dominates the scene. *(Coventry Evening Telegraph)*

9. An early disaster at Albany Road Coventry in 1904. The train was to have been used for a Swift Motor Company excursion, and those who were to have travelled on it must have been both disappointed and relieved that they weren't aboard when it ran down the embankment. Crowds have turned out to watch the recovery crane in operation. On the bridge can be seen a Webb 0-6-0 coal engine. *(Coventry City Library)*

10. A more recent mishap. This derailed coach blocked Coventry station on 21 November 1959. The engine is Stanier 2-6-2T No. 40135. Waiting in the yard is a works lorry with a shipment of well-wrapped Triumph motor bikes. In the foreground two railwaymen discuss the accident, while a group of their colleagues walk along the track towards the station. *(Coventry Evening Telegraph)*

11. A broadside shot of 'Jubilee' class No. 45555 QUEBEC taken as it leaves Coventry around 12.56 p.m. on 9 May 1955 with an express for Euston. The location is just before the line crosses the London Road, with a siding in the foreground leading to a coal merchant's yard.
(Dick Blenkinsop)

12. Fairburn 2-6-4T No. 42287 at Coventry station with the 1.50 p.m. local service to Birmingham New Street on 12 March 1965. There must be lots of people who travelled on the local train who can still repeat parrot-fashion: this is the train to Birmingham New Street calling at Canley, Tile Hill, Berkswell, Hampton-in-Arden, Marston Green, Lea Hall, Stechford, Adderley Park and Birmingham New Street. *(Ray Reed)*

13. Riddles Standard class 5MT No. 73068 with a special from Porthcawl in the summer of 1963 going to the carriage sidings at Coventry Quinton Road. *(Ray Reed)*

14. A unique road-rail bus from Lucas Aerospace poses at Coventry station in October 1984. The label in the 'destination window' reads 'LUCAS AEROSPACE COMBINED SHOPSTEWARDS COMMITTEE', and the number has been set to 007 – (licence to kill?)
(Coventry Evening Telegraph)

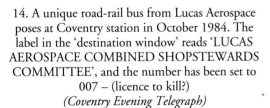

15. (left) Riddles Standard class 5MT No. 73159 at Coventry station with a football excursion train in February 1965. *(Ray Reed)*

16. (right) Ivatt 2-6-0 No. 46428 with the Nuneaton to Leamington Spa parcels train about to leave Coventry for Leamington Spa on 29 May 1965. *(Ray Reed)*

17. A brand new diesel passenger train (a Derby-built diesel multiple unit) of the type that began regular operation from Coventry on 5 March 1956. The service included daily return journeys to Birmingham, Peterborough and Leamington Spa. The total capacity of the four-coach units was 246 passengers, including 18 first class. This picture was taken in February 1956 when BR staff at Coventry station were being instructed in the operation of the new train. Stanier 2-6-2T No. 40157 can just be seen in the background. *(Coventry Evening Telegraph)*

18. Exactly ten years after the start of the new diesel service (see above), this picture (taken on 5 March 1966) shows the Birmingham Pullman at Coventry station northbound on one of its rare visits. Its duty on this occasion was as a football special to Liverpool where Coventry City (the Sky Blues) were playing away to Everton. *(Ray Reed)*

19. Chalked on the smokebox door of this redundant tanker (a Western Region Hawksworth heavy 0-6-0PT built in 1949) is the sad message 'Dr Beeching made me homeless'. It is May 1963, and the haulage company's low-loader waits in Ansty Road, Coventry, for a police escort to take it to Coventry colliery at Keresley. It was one of three (Nos. 1501, 1502 and 1509) bought by the National Coal Board for Keresley when withdrawn by British Railways. Eventually 1502 and 1509 were scrapped, but 1501 was preserved. *(Coventry Evening Telegraph)*

20. The Grosvenor Road entrance to Coventry's Warwick Road Goods Station in November 1960. *(Coventry Evening Telegraph)*

21. This photograph was taken on 20 May 1953 outside Coventry station, just visible on the right of the picture. In the foreground on Coventry shed is a Webb coal tank 2-4-2 No. 46654 shortly to be withdrawn and used on the puh-pull trains to Rugby via Leamington Spa Avenue station, and in the background 2-6-2 tank No. 40205 stands in the sidings. The 0-6-0 No. 58217 is probably shunting some coal wagons as it awaits the tall LNWR signals to change. The line to Leamington Spa leaves to the left of the picture. *(Dick Blenkinsop)*

22. Coventry shed in 1956 with former LMS 2-6-0 No. 46446 in front of an 0-8-0.
(Ray Reed)

23. Coventry shed pre-1956 with Stanier 2-6-4T No. 42541 and No. 46445 facing outwards.
(Ray Reed)

24. The old Coventry platform which was demolished in 1962. *(Coventry Evening Telegraph)*

25. Wonderful decorative ironwork at Foleshill station in the 1960s. The gate was closed for the last time in September 1962.
(Coventry Evening Telegraph)

26. The last passenger train from Coventry to Nuneaton is taken out by driver E. Prior on 18 January 1965.
(Coventry Evening Telegraph)

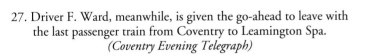

27. Driver F. Ward, meanwhile, is given the go-ahead to leave with the last passenger train from Coventry to Leamington Spa.
(Coventry Evening Telegraph)

28. On 13 February 1970 a double-decker bus crashed into the level crossing gates at Canley Halt.
(Coventry Evening Telegraph)

29. The new gates at Canley Crossing, photographed in August 1976.
(Coventry Evening Telegraph)

30. Berkswell level crossing, controlled by signalmen in Coventry, photographed in September 1982 (as a Class 47 diesel with a tank train passes) after there had been an incident involving a 49-seater coach, full of school children, which had become trapped between the barriers on the high speed line. BR spokesmen were at pains to publicly give assurance that their elaborate failsafe system had removed any danger of the coach being hit by the train.
(Coventry Evening Telegraph)

31. New safety barriers at Tile Hill station, erected in July 1979, caused annoyance amongst commuters as it was claimed they stayed down so long that many of them were missing their trains. A petition was presented to British Rail. In the picture a Class 310 EMU waits with a train to Euston. *(Coventry Evening Telegraph)*

32. The Kenilworth to Berkswell Loop has been closed for many years, and here 'Patriot' class No. 45510 has just passed Kenilworth Junction with the line curving round to cross the main Kenilworth to Coventry road. The train is the 7.55 a.m. Leamington Spa Avenue station to Liverpool Lime Street on 14 May 1955. *(Dick Blenkinsop)*

33. The 3.50 p.m. train to Rugby on 14 June 1983 was the last train to be manned by a driver and guard based at Coventry station, ending a tradition which began in 1837 when the railway first came to the city. The Coventry based crews were transferred to Rugby, Nuneaton and Birmingham New Street stations, and this photograph was taken at a farewell ceremony. *(Coventry Evening Telegraph)*

NUNEATON
and around

34. The last steam train from Trent Valley station Nuneaton pulls out on 23 April 1966 with 200 rail enthusiasts aboard for a special RCTS excursion. Locally based Ivatt 'Mogul' class 2MT 2-6-0 No. 46519 performs the final duty. *(Coventry Evening Telegraph)*

35. B1 class 4-6-0 No. 61366 from Immingham Depot on 12 July 1952 with a Saturday-only Cleethorpes to Bournemouth through train drawing away from Nuneaton Abbey station. Note the rosebay willow-herb in flower alongside the line. *(Ray Green)*

36. A Leicester to Birmingham local train hauled by LMS Compound 4-4-0 No. 41117 at Oaston crossing in June 1952. The sleepers going across the track in the foreground mark the end of Oaston Lane near to the Midland junction. The operating wire for the signal on the right ran up the outside of the post supported by brackets. *(Ray Green)*

37. Stanier 'Princess Royal' class No. 46200 THE PRINCESS ROYAL with a Euston to Glasgow train passing Ashby junction in May 1956. *(Ray Reed)*

38. LMS 4F class 0-6-0 No. 44488 leaving Nuneaton yards and crossing the main line on to the Coventry branch on 7 April 1953. The handrails in the foreground run alongside a footpath known as Birdcage Walk used by workers as a route to the loco shed from Wheat Street. *(Ray Green)*

39. With the decline in coal traffic from the Warwickshire and Leicestershire collieries, the days of Nuneaton's Trent Valley marshalling yard were numbered, and it was not long after this picture was taken in May 1968 that the yard was closed. *(Coventry Evening Telegraph)*

40. 9F 2-10-0 No. 92052 (built by BR at Crewe Works in 1955) hauls a class H freight out of Nuneaton up yard and on to the up slow line heading for Rugby in the early 1960s. The first twelve wagons contain ballast from local quarries. Although the overhead wires are in place, full semaphore signalling is still operational – behind the last ballast wagon is the signal controlling access to the up yard from the Leicester line, while behind the second wagon is the banner signal controlling the headshunt to the up yard hump. The impressive ex-LNWR 180 lever Nuneaton No. 1 signalbox is clearly seen. The relay room for the new power box is seen to the right of the locomotive. *(Martyn S. Lane)*

41. A summer Saturdays-only Paignton-Nottingham threads its way through Nuneaton Abbey Street sidings on the Birmingham-Leicester line in the mid-1960s. The train will shortly be crossing over the WCML. The yard is well filled with wagons, predominantly granite ballast from the quarry in the background. It was one of the few class 1 trains to use this line at the time, and is hauled by the latest traction in the form of 'Peak' Type 4 diesel D29, built at Derby Works in May 1961 and shedded at 17A Derby. Later renumbered 45002 in June 1963 and ultimately withdrawn from Toton depot in September 1984, it was cut up by MC Processors in Glasgow in November 1988. Passenger traffic was later diverted from this direct line through the low level WCML station. The line closed completely in 1992. *(Martyn S. Lane)*

42. A stranger from the north backs onto Nuneaton shed in the early 1960s. It would seem to have worked in on a special class 7 freight by the smokebox reporting number. No. 44118 was one of the first batch of post grouping 4F 0-6-0s to be built by the LMS to an MR design coming out of Crewe Works in 1924. The tender is very unusual as it has a roof covering the coal space which could be moved backwards and forwards on rollers for coaling purposes. It is believed that these were fitted to banking locos on the Settle & Carlisle line to prevent snow building up on the coal. *(Martyn S. Lane)*

43. Jubilee class 4-6-0 No. 45643 RODNEY wears its newly acquired 2B Nuneaton shedplate, having been relocated from 5A Crewe North shed in December 1962. The loco moved on again one year later. There appears to be a message for the fitters chalked on the cylinder cover. A tablet catcher is attached to the cabside. The loco was built at Crewe Works by the LMS in 1934. In the foreground can be seen ground shunting signals of both the old semaphore and new colour light systems. *(Martyn S. Lane)*

44. Stanier 8F 2-8-0 No. 48074 at Nuneaton sheds, with No. 48263 behind, on 18 August 1964. *(Ray Green)*

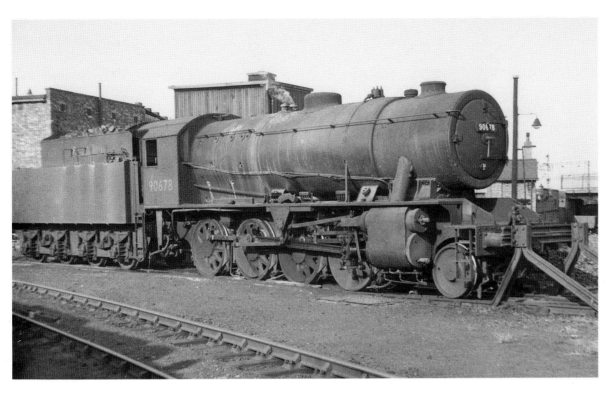

45. A rare visitor from the north-east, WD 2-8-0 No. 90678 simmers gently at the back of Nuneaton shed yard in the early 1960s. On the extreme right can be seen the bridge under the WCML through which a line ran from the shed turntable to the Leicester line, thus giving light engines access to the carriage sidings, up yard and the ex-MR Abbey Street sidings without fouling the busy main lines. *(Martyn S. Lane)*

46. Standard class 4 4-6-0 No. 75045 was one of the last residents of Nuneaton shed (then coded 5E). It is reversing into the almost deserted shed shortly before it was withdrawn from service in April 1966 – the shed closed a couple of months later. No. 75045 was built at Swindon Works in 1954 and came to Nuneaton in May 1963. *(Martyn S. Lane)*

47. The turntable at Nuneaton locomotive sheds towards the end of its days in August 1964. The maker's plate reads: 'Working load 150 tons, L. M. & S. Rly. Co. Ransomes & Rapier Ltd, Ipswich, England'. *(Ray Green)*

48. Summer 1953 at Nuneaton loco sheds. The first engine is a Lancashire and Yorkshire Rail Aspinall 0-6-0 No. 52465 and the second is LMS 4-4-0 No. 40677. Other engines in the picture are 2-6-0 'Mogul' behind hut, Stanier 8F and NW 0-8-0 in the background. *(Ray Green)*

49. Looking south from Leicester Road bridge on 3 June 1961 as Stanier class 5 4-6-0 No. 45089 approaches with fitted freight from Rugby. The houses in the background were called 'The Twelve Apostles' built in 1850 around the time the now demolished Trent Valley line was completed.

(Ray Green)

50. A lone trainspotter at Ashby junction watches Stanier class 8F 2-8-0 No. 48416 haul a heavily laden coal train towards Nuneaton from the Leicestershire coalfields in May 1956. *(Ray Reed)*

51. Stanier 'Coronation' class 4-6-2 No. 46245 CITY OF LONDON (see picture 78) at Nuneaton on the wet evening of 18 July 1964 ready to haul an up parcels and milk train. *(Ray Reed)*

53. Stanier 'Coronation' class 4-6-2 No. 46227 DUCHESS OF DEVONSHIRE at the head of the up 'Royal Scot' as it passes Nuneaton on 8 August 1953. *(Ray Green)*

52 (facing page). 'Britannia' class No. 70032 TENNYSON passing Nuneaton loco shed (on left) with the 8.30 a.m. Manchester London Road to Euston train on 28 February 1953. A goods train waits as all the signals at the approach to Nuneaton are on stop. The carriage sidings on the right are on the Nuneaton to Leicester line. The chequered board indicates a mail exchange facility. Inside the hut a man would work a mechanical arm which collected the mailbag from the passing train (this worked both ways). *(Ray Green)*

54. Hughes/Fowler 'Crab' class 2-6-0 No. 42931 passing Ashby junction with a goods train in May 1956. *(Ray Reed)*

55. A young trainspotter watches Stanier 'Jubilee' class 4-6-0 No. 45552 SILVER JUBILEE at the head of a Liverpool to Rugby passenger train passing Ashby junction in May 1956. *(Ray Reed)*

56. Ex-LNWR 0-8-0 No. 49068 passes Ashby junction in May 1956 on its way back to the Leicester collieries with an empty coal train. *(Ray Reed)*

57. On 6 June 1953 at Attleborough, Stanier 'Princess Royal' class 4-6-2 No. 46201 PRINCESS ELIZABETH hauls the up 'Merseyside Express'.
(Ray Green)

58. Rugby based LMS Compound 4-4-0 No. 41113 with a Stafford to Rugby local train passing Attleborough signalbox on 7 July 1953 on a very clean and tidy stretch of line. *(Ray Green)*

59. An up parcels train approaches Attleborough section at Nuneaton headed by a very clean 'Patriot' class 4-6-0 No. 45548 LYTHAM ST ANNES on 8 November 1952. *(Ray Green)*

60. Coton Arches viaduct, Nuneaton, on the Coventry branch, receives an engineer's inspection on 10 December 1986. The loco is 31299 built as D5832 by Brush in Loughborough in February 1962. It was withdrawn from Immingham depot in October 1990, being stored first at BSC Appleby-Frodingham works and latterly at Stratford Works. (*Martyn S. Lane*)

61. The direct Leicester to Birmingham line crossed the A444 on a low brick bridge, later replaced by a wide steel span. Stanier 8F 2-8-0 No. 48713 has left the ex-LNWR Nuneaton shed using the connection under the WCML joining the turntable to the Leicester line. It has reversed at Midland Junction and is seen heading for the ex-MR Abbey Street sidings to pick up its train. This avoided conflicting moves with the busy WCML through Nuneaton Trent Valley station. The picture was taken in early 1966. No. 48713 was transferred to Nuneaton shed from Bescot in January 1966 and was withdrawn for scrap two months later. The loco has an interesting background – built during World War II at the SR Brighton Works for the LNER where it became part of class 06 and carried the numbers 7659, 3108 and 3508. In 1946 it was sold to the LMS becoming their 8713 and later BR 48713. This line was closed to all traffic in 1992 and all trains were sent through the WCML low level station. (*Martyn S. Lane*)

62. A special train breaks through a 'welcome' banner to mark the reopening, on 10 May 1988, of Bedworth station 23 years after it had been closed – a victim of the Beeching cuts – linking it once more with the national rail network. The crowds have gathered to witness the official opening by the Mayor of Nuneaton and Bedworth and the Chairman of Warwickshire County Council, after which a party of 150 Bedworth schoolchildren travelled by train to Nuneaton and back again. The decision to reopen the station followed the earlier successful resumption of regular passenger services on the Nuneaton to Coventry line. *(Coventry Evening Telegraph)*

63. Fowler 2-6-4 tank No. 42330 with the 6.56 p.m. Nuneaton to Coventry local train arriving at Chilvers Coton station on 21 July 1953.
(Ray Green)

64. Stanier 'Coronation' class 4-6-2 No. 46251 CITY OF NOTTINGHAM at the head of the up 'Merseyside Express' as it passes Bulkington on 19 March 1954. *(Ray Green)*

65. No. 71000 up Glasgow passing Nuneaton shed on 12 November 1955. *(Ray Green)*

66. Between June 1975 and September 1978 Nuneaton was plagued with rail accidents. These pictures show the crash of 6 June 1975 when an InterCity Sleeper was derailed because the lights in a temporary speed restriction sign had failed.
(Coventry Evening Telegraph)

67. In 1957 Nuneaton Abbey Street station, for the second year running, came top in the station gardens competition and the cleanliness and tidiness competition of the Birmingham Midland district. Stanier 2-8-0 8F No. 48336 passes with a goods train while a lady tends the borders.
(Coventry Evening Telegraph)

68. A very early photograph of Abbey junction signalbox.
(Andy Walker)

RUGBY
and around

69. The entrance to Rugby Midland station in December 1959. *(Coventry Evening Telegraph)*

70. It is 10.13 a.m. on 22 November 1965 and the first of the new blue and white main line electric trains (now known as the Class 310 EMUs) arrives from London at Rugby station eight minutes ahead of schedule. This train was the forerunner of a new service from Euston which was to start in April 1966 and which would cut the journey time to Rugby by half an hour to 66 minutes. *(Coventry Evening Telegraph)*

71. Rugby's No. 1 loco shed in March 1956, the roof of which has been rebuilt to accommodate the overhead wire conductors needed for the forthcoming electrification. A Stanier class 5 4-6-0 is in the foreground. *(Coventry Evening Telegraph)*

72. More roofwork, this time in March 1961 when a major reglazing scheme was under way at Rugby Midland station.
(Coventry Evening Telegraph)

73. Ex-LNER 'V2' class 2-6-2 No. 60863 with the 'up fish' near Rugby in the 1950s. *(J.G. Click/National Railway Museum)*

74. Stanier 'Coronation' class 4-6-2 No. 46254 CITY OF STOKE-ON-TRENT with the down 'Caledonian' at Newbold water troughs.
(J.G. Click/National Railway Museum)

75 and 76. Great Central Line bridge over the Oxford Canal between Clifton and Brownsover near Rugby. Above, wooden scaffolding marks the beginning of construction in 1894. The boy leading the barge horse along the towpath is in distinct contrast to the motor-propelled working narrow boats (right) passing under the long completed bridge on 29 October 1959.
(*Rugby Library*)

77. A double-headed down express near Hillmorton with Stanier 5MT class 4-6-0 No. 44750 the leading engine. Note the Rugby radio masts in the background. *(J.G. Click/National Railway Museum)*

78. Stanier 'Coronation' class 4-6-2 No. 46245 CITY OF LONDON (see picture 51) pulling away from Rugby on the up loop line with a van train from Holyhead on 7 August 1964. The locomotive is remarkably clean considering it was due to be withdrawn a month later. At the end of its 21 years of service it had covered 1,408,315 miles. *(Derek Smith)*

79. Leaving Rugby with the 4.15 p.m. London (Euston) to Birmingham (New Street) on 1 May 1962 is Stanier Pacific 'Princess Royal' class 4-6-2 No. 46209 PRINCESS BEATRICE. The Princess Royals had been relegated to semi-fast working during their last months in service. This particular engine was withdrawn on 29 September 1962, and its total mileage since it was built in 1935 amounted to nearly 1.6m. *(Derek Smith)*

80. One of the world-renowned photographs of Rugby signals, built in 1895 and (with 44 arms) reputed to be the largest signal gantree in the British Isles – the upper set duplicating the lower. Behind the lower gantry is the Great Central Railway's Birdcage Bridge. The three left hand posts controlled trains from Blisworth, the centre five posts were for the down line from Northampton, and the group on the right applied to up trains from Market Harborough. The signals became redundant in 1939. With every signal set at danger, the 'Prince of Wales' class 4-6-0 No. 25673 LUSITANIA waits for a clear road. *(Rugby Library)*

81. Rebuilt 'Royal Scot' class 4-6-0 No. 46121 HIGHLAND LIGHT INFANTRY THE CITY OF GLASGOW REGIMENT (the longest name in the 'Royal Scot' class) of Glasgow Polmadie shed works away from Rugby in June 1960 with the up 'Mancunian'. The train had not stopped at Rugby, but with a 40 mph speed restriction through the station the engine would be working quite hard for the climb up to Hillmorton box and on to Kilsby tunnel, a further four to five miles away.
(Ray Reed)

82. It is 8 August 1961 and a rather short down fitted goods is about to pass under the well-known Wooden Bridge just north of Rugby station with Stanier 8F class 2-8-0 No. 48206 at its head. In the background is Rugby No. 5 signalbox which was demolished with the onset of electrification. *(Derek Smith)*

83. Rugby Central station in March 1963. On the back of the haulage contractor's lorry is a shipment of live yoghourt.
(Coventry Evening Telegraph)

84. A train awaits, but where are the people? The stairs down to a platform at Rugby Central station in November 1968. Six months later on 5 May 1969 passenger services ended on this line. *(Coventry Evening Telegraph)*

85. The building of the Great Central Railway between Catesby and Rugby in 1895. The first train ran in 1898. The horse pairs were used to tow away the wagons of waste soil along the already laid tracks. *(Rugby Library)*

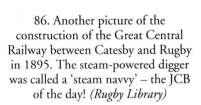

86. Another picture of the construction of the Great Central Railway between Catesby and Rugby in 1895. The steam-powered digger was called a 'steam navvy' – the JCB of the day! *(Rugby Library)*

87. Rugby goods yard in 1930 looking east. Indistinct in the background are the masts of the radio transmitter opened in 1926. *(Rugby Library)*

88. A disused coal yard at the Wood Street goods depot in September 1983. *(Coventry Evening Telegraph)*

89. Another view from Wooden Bridge, the other way this time (see picture 82), in August 1963 – a favourite haunt of trainspotters. Gantries had begun to appear to carry the overhead wires for the forthcoming electric trains. Meanwhile, the gasworks in the background had recently closed down. *(Coventry Evening Telegraph)*

90 (facing page). In this wintry scene an LNER '01' class 2-8-0 takes an up goods train over the Great Central viaduct at Rugby. *(J.G. Click/National Railway Museum)*

91. BR Riddles Standard class 2-10-0 9F No. 92132 just north of Rugby Central station on 13 February 1965 and about to take a down 'Runner' goods train across Birdcage Bridge which carried the Great Central over the London Midland. The 'Runners' or 'Windcutters' were a feature of the Great Central, and they were the fastest loose-coupled freight trains in the country, running between Annesley in Nottinghamshire and Woodford Halse. *(Derek Smith)*

92. Ex-LNER 'A3' class 4-6-2 No. 60059
TRACERY at speed with the up 'Master Cutler'
near Rugby.
(J.G. Click/National Railway Museum)

93. A Royal Observer Corps special to
Farnborough on the Great Central line near
Rugby, hauled by two Robinson LNER class 'D11'
4-4-0 locos – No. 62666 ZEEBRUGGE and
No. 62667 SOMME.
(J.G. Click/National Railway Museum)

94. A spectacular accident occurred at Barby sidings on the Eastern Region line about three miles south of Rugby at 3.10 p.m. on Sunday 7 August 1955 when a standing room only express, running 90 minutes late from Manchester to London (Marylebone), leapt off the line and down a 10 ft embankment just as it was returning to the up line from which it had been diverted at Rugby because of maintenance work. The 70-ton Gresley 2-6-2 'V2' class No. 60828 left the track, and six of the ten cream and red coaches slithered sideways, then bounced down the bank into the fields. The only fatality was the driver. *(Coventry Evening Telegraph)*

95. The recovery cranes at work after the accident.
(National Railway Museum)

96. A derailed Stanier 'Black 5' class 5MT 4-6-0 No. 44716 under Rugby's Birdcage Bridge which carries the Great Central line.
(J.G. Click/National Railway Museum)

97. An up freight near Rugby hauled by two locos, the first of which is '01' class 2-8-0 No. 63676. (*J.G. Click/National Railway Museum*)

98. As part of the BR electrification scheme the above bridge (photographed in March 1960) which crosses the London to Birmingham line near Rugby Golf Course was due for demolition. A Stanier 'Coronation' class locomotive passes underneath with the 'Midday Scot' heading for Glasgow.
(*Coventry Evening Telegraph*)

99. It is towards the end of May 1962 and Stanier 4-6-0 5MT No. 45191 fills the air with smoke and steam as if in an attempt to conceal the supports which will soon carry overhead wires past Rugby as part of the electrification of the line from London to the north. (*Coventry Evening Telegraph*)

100. 'Jubilee' class 4-6-0 No. 45644 HOWE entering Rugby on 30 March 1959 with a passenger train destined for Euston. *(Ray Reed)*

101 (above). Ex-LNER 'A4' class 4-6-2 No. 60008 DWIGHT D. EISENHOWER (in pristine condition) being towed by a '9F' class 2-10-0 through Rugby Central station past the water tower on 24 April 1964 on its way via Southampton to an enthusiast in the USA who had bought it, happily for preservation. 102 (below). Old locos lined up at Rugby Sidings in March 1960. At the front is ex-LNWR 'G2' class 7F 0-8-0 No. 49442, whose buffers bear graffiti. *(Coventry Evening Telegraph)*

104. 'V2' class 2-6-2 No. 60961 from York shed passing Rugby Central station on 27 February 1965 with a fitted goods train from Teeside to Cardiff. The loco would work as far as Woodford Halse where a GWR engine would take over for the rest of the journey. *(Derek Smith)*

103 (facing page). A down goods train is hauled through Rugby Central station by Stanier class 8F 2-8-0 No. 48003 on 13 February 1965. *(Derek Smith)*

105. 'Royal Scot' class 4-6-0 No. 46165 THE RANGER 12th LONDON REGT – minus nameplates and, in its last weeks of use, in poor external condition – waits on 11 August 1964 at Woodford Halse station on the Great Central line with a train of empty newspaper vans from Nottingham. *(Ray Reed)*

106. BR Standard class 9F No. 92244 at Woodford Halse with a fast freight on 11 August 1964. *(Ray Reed)*

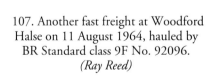

107. Another fast freight at Woodford Halse on 11 August 1964, hauled by BR Standard class 9F No. 92096. *(Ray Reed)*

108. 'U' class 2-6-0 No. 31639 pilots 'Q1' class 0-6-0 No. 33006 through Rugby and under the Birdcage Bridge with a Railtour special called 'Six Counties Rail Tour' and organized by the Home Counties Railway Society. Starting in London, it ran through Banbury to Fenny Compton where it joined the SMJR to Stratford-Upon-Avon and then on to Leamington Spa where it took the line through Marton and Birdingbury to Rugby where it seen taking the Northampton line. It then went to Wellingborough for engine turning and servicing, from where it returned to London.

(Derek Smith)

109. An S.L.S. special from Snow Hill to Woodford Halse on 24 April 1965. The train was a double header to Stratford Old Town, then class 4F 0-6-0 No. 44188 took it on to Woodford Halse. The picture shows a stop at Byfield Colliery (see pictures 163 and 164). *(Ralph Ward)*

110. Flecknoe station in the 1940s. When it closed in 1952 the buildings were moved and some went to Stockton for a cricket pavilion. If anybody has the old station sign the present owner of the land (the author) would be delighted to hear from them.

Great Central sign from an old gate near Flecknoe.

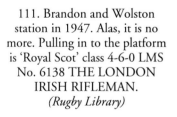

111. Brandon and Wolston station in 1947. Alas, it is no more. Pulling in to the platform is 'Royal Scot' class 4-6-0 LMS No. 6138 THE LONDON IRISH RIFLEMAN.
(Rugby Library)

112. Napton and Stockton station in the early 1900s, showing two platforms and two tracks. Just beyond the bridge to the left was the goods yard for Stockton Mill where a forfeit had to be paid if it took too long to unload the wagons.

113. A recently exposed stretch of bank on the old Great Central line looking south near the crossing of the Weedon to Leamington line at Wolfhamcote. It is said that the bank subsided in 1923 derailing an engine. As can be seen in the photograph, taken in June 1993, it was shored up by driving lengths of railway line down into the bank. *(The author)*

114. Fenny Compton in 1961 where the GWR and SMJR lines cross. The stooping railwayman takes little notice as 'King' (6000) class 4-6-0 No. 6012 KING EDWARD VI (see picture 147) powers past with the up 'Cambrian Coast Express' travelling towards Banbury. The last carriage has just passed the old Fenny Compton station. The bank in the background is no longer as seen here as there is now a marina for canal boats on that site. The track in the foreground is the SMJR line – still used for shunting work. The new signalbox is just visible in the far left of the picture.

(T.E. Williams/National Railway Museum)

115. This 0-4-0 Saddle Tank No. 8 worked for the Charwelton Quarries and was built by the Yorkshire Engine Co. in 1905. It is shown here on 12 May 1956 crossing the Priors Marston to Charwelton Road when one of the large fields near Hellidon was being mined for iron ore. The job of the man behind the loco was to stop traffic on the road when the train crossed. In between times he would wait in a hut beside the road. There is a story that, finding him asleep in front of his fire on one occasion, the engine crew, in mischievous mood, put a slate over the hut's chimney and smoked him out! *(Dick Blenkinsop)*

116. During their existence the large ironstone workings at Wroxton St Mary, just north of Banbury, ran 33 steam engines. In the 1950s names were given to the steam locos – men's first names to the six-wheelers and ladies' names to the four-wheelers. It was said that the ladies' names were those of the directors' wives, amongst whom there was no Ivy, yet the above plate was found when the works closed – perhaps a close friend.

LEAMINGTON SPA
and around

117. Bay platform and parcel sidings at Leamington Spa station on 12 August 1961. '5101' class 2-6-2T No. 5184 is on the parcel train. *(Ray Green)*

118. Prior to the installation of Colour Light Signalling, Leamington Spa had a complete set of Upper Quadrant Signals at the end of the down platform. In this photograph, taken on 18 March 1975, Class 47 No. 47473 leaves with a Poole to Newcastle. To the left are the Parish Church and the remains of the site of Avenue station before redevelopment took place. The DMU in the bay platform is for all stations to Birmingham.

(Dick Blenkinsop)

119. Stanier 'Black 5' class 5MT 4-6-0 No. 44869 leaves Leamington Spa Avenue station on 12 August 1961 to join the Great Western with an excursion train. *(Ray Green)*

120 (facing page). A two coach Stratford train with engine No. 4149, a '5101' class 2-6-2 tank, about to leave Leamington Spa on 12 August 1961. *(Ray Green)*

121. Leamington Spa looking south as Castle class 4-6-0 No. 5072 HURRICANE approaches with a return Bournemouth train on 12 August 1961. *(Ray Green)*

122. To recapture the spirit of the old Great Western Railway the *Coventry Evening Telegraph* ran a steam special from Leamington to Birmingham on 3 April 1977 hauled by 'Castle' class 4-6-0 No. 7029 CLUN CASTLE (see pictures 155 and 246). *(Coventry Evening Telegraph)*

123. '5600' class 0-6-2 tank No. 6618 near the coaling stage at Leamington Spa in August 1961. Colliery wagons went up the slope into the coaling stage, then coal was transferred by hand into small hopper wagons which, in turn, were tipped into the locomotive tenders. *(Ray Green)*

124. Another view of the coaling stage on the same day, showing also the locomotive shed.
(Ray Green)

125. The 'Birmingham Pullman' (one of the specially designed luxury Metro-Cammell diesel electric 'Blue Pullmans') drawing into Leamington station on its demonstration run on 7 September 1960. Sadly they did not prove to be the long-term success expected and were withdrawn from the Western Region service in 1973. *(Coventry Evening Telegraph)*

126. A two car Metropolitan-Cammell diesel leaving Leamington Spa Avenue station going via Kenilworth and Coventry to Nuneaton on 1 August 1964. *(Ray Green)*

127. Railway enthusiasts welcome the FLYING SCOTSMAN to Leamington station on 29 September 1968 – the famous preserved Gresley 'A3' class 4-6-2 locomotive No. 4472. *(Coventry Evening Telegraph)*

128. Two more shining examples of restored locomotives – this time of former GWR engines. In front is 'Hall' (4900) class 4-6-0 No. 5900 HINDERTON HALL (see picture 152), rescued from a breaker's yard and on its first excursion on the main line. Behind is sister locomotive 'Modified Hall' No. 6998 BURTON AGNES HALL built 18 years later in 1949. Seen at Leamington station on 15 May 1976, the train was a special; from London to Birmingham and Derby *(Coventry Evening Telegraph)*.

129. Looking north at Leamington Spa station in August 1961. The goods sidings are on the right. *(Ray Green)*

130. An early 1960s view of platforms 2 and 3 at Leamington station. *(Ray Green)*

131 and 132. The old connection from Rugby to the Great Western line at Leamington station, photographed in the early 1960s.
(Ray Green)

133. The carriage sidings and main line to Banbury at Leamington Spa, photographed in summer 1961. *(Ray Green)*

134. In winter there are few locations in Harbury Cutting where the sun reaches the lineside. Here, on 9 November 1952 below the three arch bridge, 2-6-0 No. 5370 has an empty loose-coupled coal train returning to one of the Midland coal mines. The board that the locomotive is just passing which reads 'CATCH POINTS 800 YARDS' as the up line is on a steep rising gradient. *(Dick Blenkinsop)*

Harbury Cutting, north of Fenny Compton on the Great Western line going towards Leamington Spa, was one of the longest cuttings in the world. In 1876 local newspapers reported a landslip which caused the up line to be closed for several months.

135. 'Battle of Britain' class 4-6-2 No. 34051 WINSTON CHURCHILL bursts out of Harbury Tunnel (south of Leamington Spa) on
23 May 1965 with an S.L.S. Special from Birmingham Snow Hill to Exeter and return. *(Derek Smith)*

136 (facing page). It is 21 April 1956 and, having just left the short tunnel in Harbury Cutting, R.O.D. class 2-8-0 No. 3028 has steam shut off as
it goes down the gradient to Leamington Spa some six miles away. The iron ore would have come from the Wroxton Quarries (see picture 116)
just to the north-west of Banbury. *(Dick Blenkinsop)*

137. Sunday evening 18 May 1986 and a returning special train from Stratford-upon-Avon to London passes through Harbury Cutting. This is 15 years after mainline steam running returned to British Rail, and what a magnificent sight with the former Southern Railway 'King Arthur' class 4-6-0 No. 777 SIR LAMIEL, which now is in the National Collection at York. *(Dick Blenkinsop)*

138. The world speed record holder LNER 'A4' Pacific No. 4468 MALLARD passes Greeves Sidings at Harbury Cement Works on its way south to Marylebone from York on 4 October 1986. It was to work a number of special trains to Stratford-upon-Avon that autumn. *(Dick Blenkinsop)*

139. The meeting of diesels at Whitnash just to the south of Leamington Spa at around 8.45 a.m. on 22 September 1987. The Class 50 No. 50004 ST VINCENT with a Paddington to Birmingham express and Class 58 No. 58012 works an M.G.R. coal train to Didcot Power Station. *(Dick Blenkinsop)*

140. Travelling very fast with the down 'Cambrian Coast Express' 'King' (6000) class 4-6-0 No. 6021 KING RICHARD II (see picture 144) has just passed Southam Road and Harbury station on the cold winter's morning of 2 December 1961 and the exhaust steam shows up clearly against the blue sky. The station and siding have now all been demolished and the site is used by an engineering company. *(Dick Blenkinsop)*

141. Climbing out of the Avon valley rebuilt 'Patriot' class No. 45521 RHYL is working the 7.55 a.m. Leamington Spa Avenue station to Liverpool Lime Street which ran as a stopping train to Birmingham New Street. The location is about 300 yards from where the line, now singled, crosses the Kenilworth bypass, and the date is 2 April 1952. *(Dick Blenkinsop)*

142. Great Western 'Mogul' No. 6327 passes through Warwick station with a down freight, and on the right is seen the bay platform used by the Banker for assisting goods trains up Hatton Bank when required. On this dull day of 23 January 1954 the driver has decided that he will make the climb without help. *(Dick Blenkinsop)*

143. Brush Type 4 Co-Co Class 47 D1717 on the up 'Cambrian Coast Express' on 1 August 1964 approaching Leamington Spa having passed under the aqueduct three-quarters of a mile north of Leamington GWR station. The diesel is about to pass a linesmen's hut which, but for a leaning chimney, is in notably good order. D1717 was given the name of THE COMMONWEALTH SPIRIT in April 1979. *(Ray Green)*

144. Warwick goods yard used to be a busy place, but even in 1962 there was not much traffic and it has now been covered with buildings right up to the two running lines. No. 6021 KING RICHARD II (see picture 140) has just passed through the station with the 9.10 a.m. Paddington to Birkenhead express on 17 March 1962. Note the smoke from the Banker in the bay platform. *(Dick Blenkinsop)*

146. This viaduct takes the Coventry to Leamington Spa line over the River Avon and is now mostly single line but used extensively by British Rail InterCity. Class 47 No. 47471 NORMAN TUNNA GC has a short train from Paddington to Liverpool on 24 April 1984.
(Dick Blenkinsop)

145 (facing page). An up freight hauled by 'Castle' (4073) class 4-6-0 No. 4092 DUNRAVEN CASTLE on the old Great Western line at Budbrooke, near Warwick, on 28 March 1959. *(T.E. Williams/National Railway Museum)*

147. 'King' (6000) class 4-6-0 No. 6012 KING EDWARD VI (see picture 114) speeds over Hatton Bank on 23 April 1962. *(Ray Green)*

Mr Ray Green and his wife spent the day at Hatton Bank on 23 April 1962. Because of rebuilding work at Birmingham New Street station LNWR line trains were being diverted through Snow Hill station onto the Great Western line. This promised a train almost every half hour over Hatton Bank and made the 23 mile cycle ride from Nuneaton well worthwhile.

148. 'Hall' class No. 7905 FOWEY HALL piloting 'Castle' (4073) class No. 5067 ST FAGANS CASTLE as the Saturdays-only Hastings to Wolverhampton ascends Hatton Bank on 23 April 1962. *(Ray Green)*

149. Heading along Hatton Bank is 'Castle' (4073) class 4-6-0 No. 5034 CORFE CASTLE with the 3.35 p.m. train out of Wolverhampton.
(Ray Green)

150. Ascending Hatton Bank on 23 April 1962 with the 11.40 a.m. Birkenhead to Paddington is 'King' (6000) class 4-6-0 No. 6008 KING JAMES II. *(Ray Green)*

151. The 3.10 p.m. Paddington to Wolverhampton ascends Hatton Bank worked by 'King' (6000) class 4-6-0 No. 6027 KING RICHARD I on 23 April 1962. *(Ray Green)*

152 (facing page). With the train comprising all Great Western coaches in chocolate and cream livery and hauled by No. 7808 COOKHAM MANOR and 5900 HINDERTON HALL (see picture 128), this marvellous sight was recorded at the foot of Hatton Bank near Budbrook. It was a special train from the Didcot Railway Centre, home of the Great Western Society, to Stratford-upon-Avon on 6 October 1979. *(Dick Blenkinsop)*

153. '5700' class 0-6-0PTs Nos. 9630 and 9610 (see picture 184) passing an unchanged Hatton station heading for Leamington Spa with an S.L.S. special 'Farewell to GWR Panniers' on 11 September 1966. *(Ralph Ward)*

154. Hatton station, all character gone and now reduced in size to just a footbridge and a small booking office, reverberates to the sound of 'Merchant Navy' class Pacific No. 35028 CLAN LINE on a northbound excursion on 11 July 1987. *(Dick Blenkinsop)*

155. On a trial run on 7 June 1972 prior to an open day at Tyseley the following Sunday, No. 7029 CLUN CASTLE (see pictures 122 and 246) steams into Hatton station. *(Coventry Evening Telegraph)*

156. This is a typical local train of the 1950s running from Leamington Spa to Birmingham and hauled here by 2-6-2T '5101' class No. 5184 on the summer evening of 7 June 1957. It has just passed Hatton North signalbox, seen in the background, and the fine set of Great Western signals. The left signal controls the entry to the goods loop before the station, the two in the off position the 'up main' (awaiting the 6 p.m. Birmingham-Paddington) and the two on the right control the junction for the Stratford-upon-Avon line. *(Dick Blenkinsop)*

157. A down express near Hatton on 22 August 1953 hauled by '4300' class 2-6-0 No. 6391. *(T.E. Williams/National Railway Museum)*

158. It is 8 October 1952 on the GWR line at Hatton and a clean '2800' class 2-8-0 engine No. 2883 works hard with a down freight. The three-arch bridge near Hatton Craft Centre can be seen in the background. *(T.E. Williams/National Railway Museum)*

159. Ex-GWR '2800' class 2-8-0 No. 2830 hauling unfitted freight over the water troughs near Lapworth in April 1957.
(T.E. Williams/National Railway Museum)

160. Taken from the bridge shown in the picture opposite, this photograph is of 'Castle' (4073) class 4-6-0 No. 5075 WELLINGTON with the Ramsgate to Birkenhead through train on 19 June 1954 taking on water and with its tender about to overflow. The supply tank for the water troughs is on the left. The scene today is radically changed as the M40 has carved its way through the hill to the right of the telegraph poles.

(Dick Blenkinsop)

STRATFORD-UPON-AVON
and around

161. Restored 'Castle' (4073) class 4-6-0 No. 5029 NUNNEY CASTLE, to the excitement of the throng of onlookers, pulls into Stratford station with the special 'Shakespeare Express' from London on Saturday 9 November 1991. *(Paul Gilroy/Coventry Evening Telegraph)*

162. The Stratford-upon-Avon and Midland Junction Railway loco shed and station at Stratford on 22 March 1957. In the foreground is the line to Broom Junction, and on the far left is the branch line connecting with the GWR line. *(T.E. Williams/National Railway Museum)*

164 (left). Another photograph of No. 44188 further along the line as it crosses the Oxford Canal near Claydon on its way to Woodford Halse with the S.L.S. Special. *(Dick Blenkinsop)*

165 (below). The same place as above at 8.30 a.m. on 16 April 1993, and participants in an Outward Bound managerial training course are having to cross the canal without the aid of the bridge, long since removed. *(The author)*

163 (facing page). Fowler 4F class 0-6-0 No. 44188 steams by at Northend, between Kineton and Fenny Compton, with a Special organized by the Stephenson Locomotive Society on 24 April 1965 to mark the closure of the Stratford-upon-Avon and Midland Junction Railway line. This last passenger train on the SMJR line had run down from Birmingham to Stratford-upon-Avon double-headed with 0-6-0PT '6400' class No. 6435, which was then detached leaving No. 44188 to carry on along the SMJR line to Woodford Halse and return alone. *(Derek Smith)*

166 (left). Just west of Fenny Compton is this bridge – originally built to allow for a double track – over which goes the small section of the old SMJR line still being used by rail traffic from Fenny Compton to MOD Kineton. The bridge that can be seen in the distance is a farm bridge which still today carries the ex-GWR main line between London and Birmingham.

167 (below left). This boundary marker stands between the old GWR and SMJR lines near Fenny Compton.

168 (below right). This rather shot-up marker board is nailed to a tree along the route of the old SMJR (later LMS) line.

169. Taken on 17 April 1931 this photograph of the old Edge Hill Light Railway, which hauled stone down Edgehill to the SMJR up until 1925, shows 0-6-0 No. 2 LBSC 74/674 SHADWELL (built in 1872). The ex-GER brake van was scrapped in 1946 by J. Friswell and Sons of Banbury. *(National Railway Museum)*

170. Looking north down the incline of the old Edge Hill Light Railway on 2 October 1942 showing the beginning of the three-rail section. *(National Railway Museum)*

171. The derelict Edge Hill Light Railway sidings at the foot of the incline looking north-west on 14 July 1942. Two abandoned tank engines, a brake van and the remains of tipping wagons soak up the heat of a summer's day, while in the field nearby horses provide the traction for a local farmer. *(National Railway Museum)*

172. Looking up the same incline as it is today. *(The author)*

The MOD's Central Ammunition Depot at Kineton is at the present end of the old SMJR. This first started operation in October 1942 at Marlborough Farm Camp (it was at Marlborough Farm that the Edgehill Light Railway used to join the SMJR). The Kineton depot also provides secure accommodation and storage for over 180 BR vehicles, many of which belong to InterCity and the Parcels sectors of BR. In 1974 the area contained 93 miles of track, but since a rebuild this has been reduced to about 42 miles.

173. Everywhere spick and span Army fashion for the Open Day to mark Central Ammunition Depot's 50th Anniversary on 8 October 1992. An InterCity liveried Class 47 No. 47558 MAYFLOWER stands at the head of three matching parcel vans Nos. 95400, 95410 and 92242 with Res-liveried class 47 No. 47531 at the rear. Class 55 'Deltic' No. 55015 TULYAR in the far background was one of the star attractions.

174. Kineton has its own locomotive depot where its fleet of diesels is kept in superb condition. Here, staff take a photocall at MOD Kineton in front of locomotive Nos. 278 COPPICE, 277 EDGEHILL and 274 WAGGONER all built by Thomas Hill in 1987/88.

175. In 1989 a rail spur to a shed at MOD Kineton was being removed by contractors and, although the fish plates had been removed, the points were inadvertently left pulled for the shed spur and an MOD diesel engine and four wagons became derailed. In turn a 25 ton jack was used to lift the loco and the wagons, and by pressure from a side jack they were pushed and toppled back onto the track, and in less than six hours.
(I.G.M. Pardoe collection)

176. The derelict platform at Shipston-on-Stour photographed in November 1961. Regular passenger services to and from this station, at the end of a branch line from the old Stratford and Moreton Railway, ceased in 1929. *(Coventry Evening Telegraph)*

177. '2884' class 2-8-0 No. 3809 passing through the countryside near Honeybourne with an up freight train on 7 March 1964.
(*T.E. Williams/National Railway Museum*)

178 (left). The original 1883 Great Western footbridge at Wilmcote station, 110 years old and still looking good. *(The author)*

179 (right). Summer evening sunshine filters through the latticework of the old GWR bridge at Wilmcote – a welcome sight for travellers returning home from a long day's work. *(The author)*

180. Ex-GWR 'Castle' (4073) class 4-6-0 No. 5079 LYSANDER takes a photo call as it slowly crosses the points on to the grassy Bearley North to Bearley East Junction curve with an up express that had been diverted via the North Warwickshire line on Sunday 24 May 1959. The bridge in the background is the aqueduct carrying the Stratford-upon-Avon canal over the line (see picture opposite).
(T.E. Williams/National Railway Museum)

181. The signalbox at Bearley West Junction photographed on 12 November 1984 when the four-mile section of the old North Warwickshire Railway line between Bearley and Henley-in-Arden was under threat of closure. The Bearley West box is still in operation today.
(S. Douglass/Coventry Evening Telegraph)

182. A very lucky photograph of a canal boat crossing the railway on the Bearley Aqueduct as 'V2' class LNER No. 4771 GREEN ARROW comes underneath with a Locomotive Club of Great Britain special. It was returning from Stratford-upon-Avon to Birmingham on the North Warwickshire line on 10 June 1973, and the locomotive is, of course, part of the National collection. *(Dick Blenkinsop)*

183. Familiarity with the train timetable and an accurate watch would seem to be essentials for this farmer who regularly crossed the North Warwickshire line with his herd of 70 Friesian cattle near Wootton Wawen. The photograph, taken in December 1970, also shows the Bearley Aqueduct in the background. At the approaches to the crossing British Railways had installed trackside 'whistle' signs, but how do you hurry a herd of cows? *(Coventry Evening Telegraph)*

184. Two '5700' class tanks, Nos. 9630 and 9610 (see picture 153), leave Henley-in-Arden station heading for Leamington Spa with a Stephenson Locomotive Society 'farewell to GWR panniers' special on 11 September 1966. *(Ralph Ward)*

185. GWR style still as it was. This photograph was taken in May 1993. *(The author)*

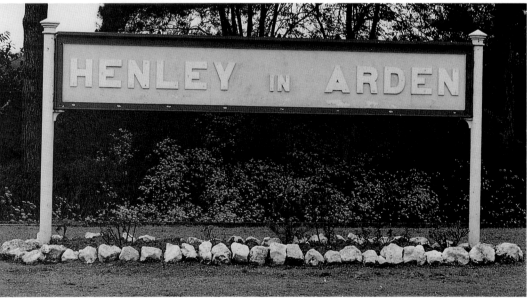

GLOUCESTERSHIRE WARWICKSHIRE RAILWAY

186. On loan from the Severn Valley Railway, preserved Ivatt No. 46521 takes on water at Toddington station on the preserved Gloucestershire Warwickshire Railway line in April 1993. Ian Coull was the driver and Pat Walker the fireman. *(The author)*

187. The 'dashboard' of Ivatt No. 46521. *(The author)*

188. Preserved Fowler 0-6-0T LMS No. 7298 at Toddington station ready for a Gloucestershire Warwickshire Railway excursion. *(The author)*

189. Built originally for the Army, this special rail-going S-type Bedford lorry was used for hauling wagons when no locomotive was available. It has a normal gearbox, so forward movement can be quite fast, but with only one reverse gear it means that in the absence of a turntable any return trip is a good deal slower. It is now part of the Gloucestershire Warwickshire Railway collection. (The author)

190. A restored LMS brakevan ex-Hunts of Hinkley (the lemonade people) now in the collection at Gloucestershire Warwickshire Railway at Toddington. (The author)

191. Baguley-Drewry railcar No. 9127 (built at Burton-on-Trent in 1976) is seen at the GWR depot at Toddington where it is used by the 'permanent way' and 'signal and telegraph' departments. It worked at MOD Kineton from 1977 to 1991 when it was donated to GWR Ltd complete with a trailer and flat wagon. It is powered by a 68 bhp Perkins diesel engine. The trailer was itself a railcar – originally No. 9119 – and this is being converted for use by the GWR depot's fire brigade. *(Steve Standbridge)*

192. Rescued general purpose goods van from pre-grouping days – also part of the GWR collection. Note the loose-coupled braking system. *(The author)*

Bagnall 0-6-0ST No. 2655 'Byfield No. 2' was originally ordered by the Ministry of Supply as a batch of six intended for mineral works in the Midlands, and was delivered to Byfield stone quarries in February 1942. The quarry was closed temporarily in 1944 and No. 2 was moved to Wroxton St Mary quarries. In January 1947 it was sold to Loddington Ironstone Co. and renamed Loddington No. 2. In 1961 it came into the ownership of Staveley Minerals Ltd and after being moved to Cranford quarries as a standby in 1966 it was sold, four years later, to Hunt and Co. (Hinkley) Ltd, from whom Gloucester Warwickshire Railway bought it in April 1986 and have since kept it in working order.

193. Looking rather neglected at Cranford around 1968/1969. *(Pat Walker)*

194. At work for the Gloucestershire Warwickshire Railway on Sunday 8 July 1990, coming out of Greet tunnel near Gretton. *(Wayne Finch)*

195. On temporary duty at the Central Ammunition Depot at Kineton to where it was transported by road to take part in the 50th Anniversary celebrations in October 1992. This was the first time a steam locomotive had run on the depot system for 30 years.

BIRMINGHAM
and around

196. Waiting for the off (northwards) on 9 August 1963 at Birmingham New Street station are ex-LMS Stanier 'Black 5' class 4-6-0 No. 44814, and ex-LNER Thompson 'B1' class 4-6-0 No. 61169. *(Ray Reed)*

Many of the photographs in this book, particularly in this section, are by Mr Ray Reed who retired in March 1993 after working for British Railways at Coventry for 44 years. During the late 1950s and early 1960s he was a keen photographer of 'steam' and spent many Saturday afternoons at Birmingham with his camera.

197. 'Jubilee' class 4-6-0 No. 45682 TRAFALGAR arrives at Birmingham New Street with the 12.15 p.m. from York in October 1956. *(Ray Reed)*

198. It is 28 March 1959 and Stanier 'Black 5' 4-6-0 No. 45064 waits to take a passenger train from New Street to Euston, while 'Jubilee' class 4-6-0 No. 45709 IMPLACABLE arrives from Euston. *(Ray Reed)*

199. The sunny Saturday afternoon of 25 July 1959 sees Hughes/Fowler 'Crab' class 2-6-0 No. 42826 waiting under the magnificent curved roof of Birmingham New Street station. *(Ray Reed)*

201 (facing page). Stanier 'Jubilee' class 4-6-0 No. 45623 PALESTINE arrives at New Street with a train from Euston on 25 July 1959. *(Ray Reed)*

200. 'Black 5' No. 44919 standing by at Birmingham New Street on 9 August 1963. The building going up in the background is the Rotunda. *(Ray Reed)*

203. Stanier 'Black 5' class 4-6-0
No. 45111 leaving New Street with
empty stock on 4 June 1960.
(Ray Reed)

204. Stanier 'Jubilee' class 4-6-0 No. 45647
STURDEE at New Street on 8 August 1959.
(Ray Reed)

202 (facing page). Standing on the middle rails
and looking very clean, Rebuilt Fowler 'Royal
Scot' class 4-6-0 No. 46148 THE
MANCHESTER REGIMENT waits to
proceed on 14 April 1962 at New Street
station. *(Ray Reed)*

205. Stanier 'Jubilee' class 4-6-0 No. 45736 PHOENIX at New Street's platform 3 in the late 1950s waiting to start its next duty. *(Ray Reed)*

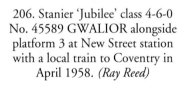

206. Stanier 'Jubilee' class 4-6-0 No. 45589 GWALIOR alongside platform 3 at New Street station with a local train to Coventry in April 1958. *(Ray Reed)*

207. 'Jubilee' 4-6-0 No. 45742 CONNAUGHT waits at New Street platform 3 on 8 August 1959 with a train to Euston. The old station walkway can be seen clearly in the background. The entrance was through the buildings on the right, where facilities included a large taxi rank, a tobacconist's kiosk and a ladies hairdresser.
(Ray Reed)

208. LMS 'Compound' 4-4-0 No. 41122 arriving at New Street's platform 3 to form the 3.55 p.m. Eastern Counties to Coventry, Rugby, Market Harborough and beyond.
(Ray Reed)

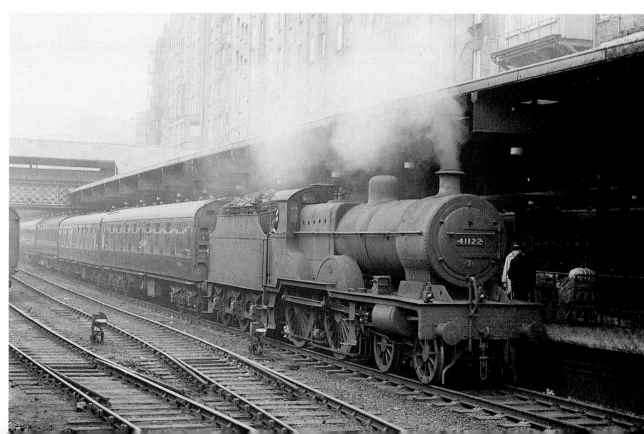

209. Ex-LMS Fowler 'Patriot' class 4-6-0 No. 45546 FLEETWOOD at New Street on 12 August 1961 with a train from the north-west. *(Ray Reed)*

210. Under close inspection from a group of enthusiastic schoolboy trainspotters is LNWR 0-8-0 No. 48930 while it waits at New Street at the head of a Stephenson Locomotive Society special excursion train due for a trip around the Birmingham area on 2 June 1962. *(Ray Reed)*

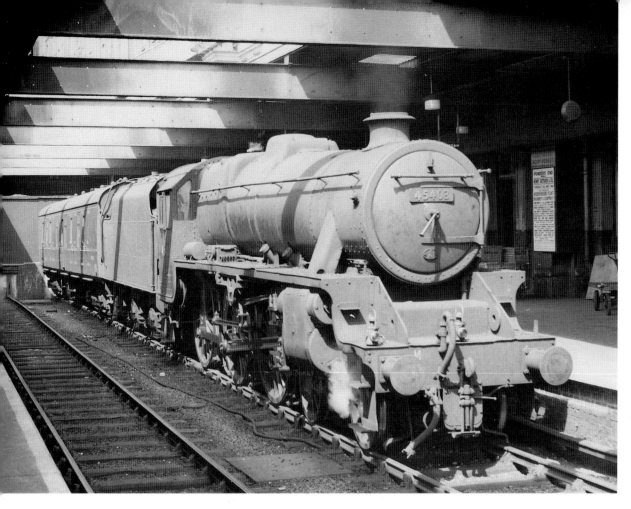

211. Stanier 4-6-0 5MT No. 45403 standing in a bay at New Street on 22 July 1961 enjoying the sunshine, just like an old dog lying on the lawn. The locomotive is under steam, though, so duty was soon to call. *(Ray Reed)*

212. Riddles 'Britannia' class 7 Pacific No. 70004 WILLIAM SHAKESPEARE about to leave New Street platform 3 on 29 August 1961 with a relief service train for Euston made up from old LNER coaches. *(Ray Reed)*

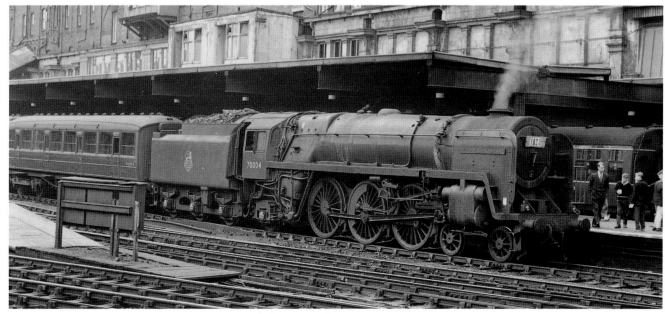

213. The arrival of No. 73068 at New Street station with a train from the West Country on 27 May 1959 is insufficient to attract the attention of all the waiting figures on the platform. *(Ray Reed)*

214. The 'Devonian' arrives at New Street after the long haul from Kingswear headed by 'Jubilee' class 4-6-0 No. 45662 KEMPENFELT on 16 April 1960, but journey's end isn't until it reaches Bradford after calling at Leeds. *(Ray Reed)*

215. It's a bleak 26 January 1957, and amidst clouds of steam in the cold air Stanier 'Black 5' 4-6-0 No. 45308 departs from New Street as it continues its journey from York to Bristol via Lickey Bank. Meanwhile two Birmingham Corporation buses cross Hill Street bridge above.
(Ray Green)

216. The entrance to Birmingham's Snow Hill station through the old GWR Hotel in Colmore Row as seen on 7 September 1963. Demolition of the building began towards the end of 1969, after main line services through the once great station had ceased in 1967. The station was eventually rebuilt and was officially reopened on 2 October 1987. *(Ray Green)*

217. The entrance to the new Snow Hill station in Birmingham photographed on 13 May 1993. BR's sign marking the entrance to an elevated walkway is dwarfed by massive office blocks. *(The author)*

218. '5700' class 0-6-0 pannier tank No. 9614 from Snow Hill hauls a mixed and very long goods train from Hockley to Bordesley. *(Ray Green)*

219. Ex-GWR '5700' class 0-6-0 pannier tank No. 4635 passing Snow Hill station on 19 October 1964 with a local goods train. *(Ray Reed)*

220. A passenger train bound for Paddington waits for the off at Snow Hill station headed by 'Castle' (4073) class 4-6-0 No. 5008 RAGLAN CASTLE in August 1957. *(Ray Reed)*

221. No. 7918 RHOSE WOOD HALL at Snow Hill with empty coaching stock in August 1957. *(Ray Reed)*

222. A Talyllyn Railway Special headed by 'Battle of Britain' class 4-6-2 No. 34064 FIGHTER COMMAND at Snow Hill. *(Ray Reed)*

223. Attentive young trainspotters watch the passage through Snow Hill station of '9F' class 2-10-0 No. 92218 with a cement train on 19 October 1964. *(Ray Reed)*

224. Collett 'Castle' (4073) class 4-6-0 No. 5065 NEWPORT CASTLE arriving at Snow Hill station's platform 7 with the up 'Cambrian Coast Express' at 4 p.m. on 4 August 1959. The station roof is a sight to behold. *(Ray Green)*

225. Collett 'King' (6000) class 4-6-0 No. 6020 KING HENRY IV arriving at Snow Hill with the Birkenhead to Paddington train at 3 p.m. on 26 January 1957. *(Ray Green)*

226. Churchward '2800' class 2-8-0 No. 2804 pulls a through freight train past the north signalbox (since demolished) at Snow Hill on 26 January 1957. *(Ray Green)*

227. '4575' class 2-6-2 tank No. 5518 arriving with a local train at Snow Hill station on 26 January 1957. *(Ray Green)*

228. All white but, sadly, not all right. D 0260 LION, a prototype 2,750 hp Co-Co Type diesel-electric – built by AEI, Sulzer Bros and the Birmingham Railway Carriage & Wagon Company – put in some impressive test times, but after being handed over to British Railways at Smethwick towards the end of May 1962 for use between Wolverhampton and Paddington it failed in service and lost its place to its rival – Brush Electrical Engineering's prototype 2,800 hp FALCON. Here LION is seen tackling the Lickey incline with a 16 coach train before the handover. *(Sulzer Bros)*

229. All that is left of one of the largest goods stations in the country. We should be thankful that the Philip Hardwick designed central block, once the Victoria Hotel at the entrance to what was the London & Birmingham Railway Curzon Street terminus, has not suffered the same fate as its big brother at Euston. *(The author)*

230/231. Moor Street station, old and new. In the old station (above) there are posters calling for help to preserve the site as it is. Just beyond this gate there was a unique piece of track that enabled engines arriving at the terminus in front of their carriages to be moved sideways so that they were then free to reverse out of the station. Both photographs taken in May 1993.
(The author)

232/233. Horses used to be part of the railway scene; their job being to cart goods to and from local customers. These two pictures, taken at the Midland Railway Company's Lawley Street station on 30 June 1909, and so obviously posed, show the pride the railway companies took in their animals. In the photograph to the left the rear grey (wheeler) sports a plume on top of his bridle, and three shiny brasses on his brisket strap. The wheeler has a heavy protective pad for the chain that holds the shafts up, whilst the lead horse only needs a light strap to hold the chains in the correct place. *(National Railway Museum)*

234. Stanier 'Black 5' 4-6-0 No. 45268 passing Water Orton with a goods train going towards Birmingham in May 1957. *(Ray Reed)*

235. The 9.30 a.m. freight train, headed by ex-LNWR 0-8-0 No. 49430 (see picture 240), passes between Water Orton and Wolverhampton on a cold and misty 29 February 1964. *(Ray Reed)*

236. Young enthusiasts gather at Park Lane junction outside Water Orton to watch a British Railways 'Britannia' Pacific hauling a Warwick Railway Society special on 27 November 1966. *(Ray Reed)*

237. It's the only way to travel! The crew of Stanier 2-8-0 8F No. 48109 are not quite sure what to make of Mr Dick Pashley's pedal-powered 'railway quadcycle' as it sweeps past them at 15 mph with its glamorous passenger sitting in her personal first-class compartment. It is May 1963 at Whitacre station and Mr Pashley, a director of the Birmingham cycle firm of W.R. Pashley and Sons Ltd, demonstrates his machine, several tandem versions of which were in use for ganging work on the railways of Southern Ireland. *(Coventry Evening Telegraph)*

238. The former level-crossing gatehouse of the old Birmingham and Derby Junction Railway, near Maxstoke Castle on the Tamworth to Hampton line in May 1971. As the *Coventry Evening Telegraph* referred to it: 'a splendid piece of "railway-ecclesiastical" architecture.'
(Coventry Evening Telegraph)

239. Ex-Southern Region 'Battle of Britain' class 4-6-2 No. 34079 141 SQUADRON at Walsall on 14 June 1964 with a Warwick Railway Society organized enthusiasts' special returning from Crewe. *(Ray Reed)*

240. Ex-LNWR 7F 0-8-0 No. 49430 (see picture 235) hauling a goods train at Bescot, near Walsall, on 10 August 1964. In the background can be seen part of the M6 under construction. The stripe on the side of the locomotive's cab was to indicate that it could not be used under the overhead electric wires. *(Ray Reed)*

241. A goods train passes the GWR signalbox at Tyseley station going south towards Warwick on the Great Western line on 6 November 1965. The line going to the right is the North Warwickshire Railway. The fluttering clothes lines in the gardens backing on to the track clearly show that it was wash day, but whether things stayed clean with all the smoke and smuts from passing trains is another matter. *(Ralph Ward)*

242 (facing page). The roundhouse shed at Tyseley had capacity for 28 locomotives arranged in a circle around a central turntable. This photograph, taken on 16 December 1956, shows it in good order. The facing engines are 'R.O.D.' class 2-8-0 No. 3018 and Collett 'Hall' (4900) class 5MT 4-6-0 No. 6904 CHARFIELD HALL. *(Ray Green)*

243. 'R.O.D.' class 2-8-0 No. 3018 from a different angle in Tyseley roundhouse shed on 16 December 1956. *(Ray Green)*

244. Another interior shot of Tyseley roundhouse shed in December 1956. On the far left is '5101' class 2-6-2T No. 5156, and the three '5700' class 0-6-0 pannier tanks are Nos. 7763, 3693 and 7713. *(Ray Green)*

245. Nine years later, on 6 November 1965, Tyseley roundhouse is beginning to look a bit ramshackle. The dilapidated panels, nevertheless, lend an atmosphere to this scene as they split the winter sunshine into a myriad shafts of light, silhouetting two '5600' class 0-6-2 tanks Nos. 6625 and 5658, while the light hits a '9F' class 2-10-0 on the left. *(Ralph Ward)*

246 (above). It is open day at Tyseley Motive Power Depot in summer 1970 and the scene is photographed through a broken window in the then derelict, and shortly to be demolished, roundhouse. The coaling plant and water tower can be seen on the left, while on the right waits the push-pull train powered by No. 7029 CLUN CASTLE (see pictures 122 and 155) and 'Jubilee' class No. 5593 KHOLAPUR which would have steamed up and down from Tyseley station to the depot. *(Ralph Ward)*

247. All that now remains of the famous roundhouse at Tyseley. The turntable is still being used by preserved engines and carriages. *(The author)*

248. Standing outside Tyseley shed on a damp16 December 1956, looking from the shed towards the road in front of the station, are '2884' class 2-8-0 No. 3808, '4300' class 2-6-0 No. 6384 and BR Standard class 5MT 4-6-0 No. 73036. The area is now a car park for the railway museum.
(Ray Green)

249. A watercolour by S. Martin 1883 of the arrival at Solihull station of the Warwickshire Hounds eager to join the waiting hunt after their journey in a travelling van from their kennels at Kineton. Just above the uniformed porter, holding open the van door, is the 'GW' sign.

250. The large Birmingham engineering works used to close for two weeks each year for the summer break, and on such occasions in the 50s and 60s New Street station was packed with families heading for their annual holidays by the sea in Somerset, Devon or Cornwall. Back on the train at the end of the fortnight, it was on reaching the Lickey incline to wait for an extra push from the bankers that they knew the holiday was really over. The photograph shows ex-GWR '9400' class 0-6-0 pannier tank No. 8405 and ex-LMS Fowler 0-6-0 3F tank No. 47308 on banking duty for 'The Devonian' en route from Paignton to Bradford on 17 May 1958. *(T.E. Williams/National Railway Museum)*

INDUSTRIAL LOCOMOTIVES
Compiled and edited by R.D. Darvill

Warwickshire has always had a large variety of industrial railway systems, from quarries and collieries through to the power stations, gas works and heavy engineering of the Birmingham conurbation. Regretfully, most of these systems have now closed, but the following selection of photographs shows the varied types of locomotives which have worked within the county.

251. Rugby Cement, New Bilton Works, Rugby. Horse drawn railways existed for many years, and this picture is believed to have been taken in the late nineteenth century. It shows a narrow gauge system which was used to bring stone from the quarry to the works. Some wonderful headgear is in evidence. *(Rugby Cement)*

252. A lithographic view of the Rugby Cement New Bilton Works at the turn of the century. The Birmingham to London line, and the West Coast main line, can be seen in the background. *(Rugby Cement)*

253. Rugby Cement, Southam Works. TRIASSIC Peckett 1270 of 1911 standing at the coaling point inside the works. This locomotive worked the 1' 11¹/₂" gauge quarry system, and after its closure was acquired for preservation, and can now be found at a private site in Surrey.
(Industrial Railway Society/K.J. Cooper Collection)

254. Rugby Cement, Southam Works. LIASSIC Peckett 1632 of 1923 awaiting its next turn of duty outside the narrow gauge shed on 27 October 1956. This was another locomotive acquired for preservation but, as it was exported to Canada in 1959, quite a journey will have to be made to see this locomotive again.
(Industrial Railway Society/B. Mettam Collection)

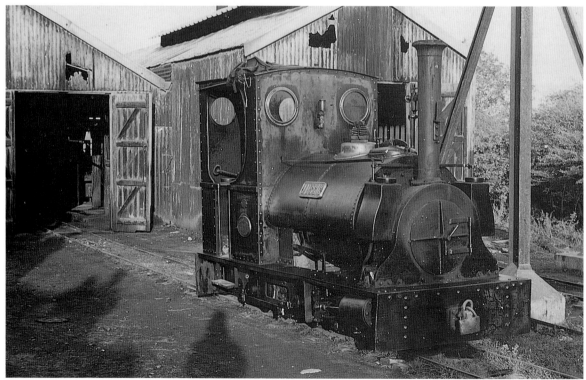

255. Rugby Cement, New Bilton Works, Rugby. Manning Wardle 2047 of 1926, the last ever locomotive to be built by this firm, stands in the yard on 18 March 1961 with driver Bill Curtis in attendance. The locomotive can now be seen on the Severn Valley Railway at Bridgnorth, Shropshire. *(Industrial Railway Society/K.J. Cooper Collection)*

256. Rugby Cement, New Bilton Works, Rugby. Robert Stephenson & Hawthorn 7387 of 1948 working on 27 March 1951. Regretably, this locomotive did not last for many years, being cut up for scrap in March 1966. *(Industrial Railway Society/K.J. Cooper Collection)*

257. Jee's Hartshill Granite, Nuneaton. Working on the unusual gauge of 2' 6½" STAFFORD Bagnall 1911 of 1912 is seen here on 25 October 1952. The rail system was abandoned in 1954, and the locomotive was cut up for scrap.
(Industrial Railway Society/K.J. Cooper Collection)

258. Man-Abell Quarries, Hartshill. DOT Bagnall 2214 of 1925 working through the fields on the 3' 0" gauge quarry system.
(Industrial Railway Society/K.J. Cooper Collection)

259. Man-Abell Quarries, Mancetter. Another unusual gauge was used here – 2' 8$^{1}/_{2}$", and OLDBURY Hunslet 754 of 1901 stands out in the yard in 1952. The locomotive only lasted for another three years before being scrapped. *(Industrial Railway Society/K.J. Cooper Collection)*

260. APCM Ufton Lime Pits. Ruston & Hornsby 281290 of 1949, a Type 100DL, 3' 0" gauge locomotive; busy in the quarry on 5 November 1950. After spells of work at other sites around the country, the locomotive is now preserved at the Irchester Country Park, Northamptonshire. *(Industrial Railway Society/K.J. Cooper Collection)*

261. Arley Colliery. JOAN Avonside 2048 of 1932, in very well kept condition, poses in the colliery yard on 5 March 1967 shortly before its transfer to Newdigate Colliery.
(Industrial Railway Society/J. Hill Collection)

262. Baddesley Colliery. Only three Garratt locomotives were built for industrial service in Britain, and the last of these to see use was WILLIAM FRANCIS Beyer Peacock 6841 of 1937. It was used to take coal to the sidings adjacent to the West Coast main line, and crossed over the A5 just north of Atherstone. It is seen here in the sidings on 16 September 1963. The locomotive is now preserved at Bressingham Hall, Norfolk.
(Industrial Railway Society/B. Mettam Collection)

263. Baddesley Colliery. Rolls Royce 10255 of 1966, a 325 hp locomotive, pulls a rake of loaded wagons through the yard on 29 October 1980. The colliery was closed in March 1989 and the locomotive transferred to Lea Hall Colliery, Staffordshire. *(A.J. Booth)*

264. Birch Coppice Colliery. Another very smart locomotive, JOHN ROBERT Manning Wardle 1891 of 1916 is seen here on 25 August 1962 just after its arrival from Baddesley. Despite its good condition it was scrapped just four years later. *(Industrial Railway Society/K.J. Cooper Collection)*

265. Birch Coppice Colliery. BIRCH COPPICE Hunslet 1637 of 1929 spent its entire life at the colliery, and is photographed here on 23 June 1963. With the advent of the diesels it only lasted another three years before being sent away for scrap. *(Industrial Railway Society/K.J. Cooper Collection)*

266. Coventry Colliery. COVENTRY No. 5 Sharp Stewart 3449 of 1888, a very nice looking large locomotive which was originally built for the Barry Railway as their No. 1; it also saw service on the GWR as No. 699. It arrived at the colliery in 1933 and lasted until 1962 before being scrapped by Jacksons. *(Industrial Railway Society/K.J. Cooper Collection)*

267. Coventry Homefire Plant. Being hired to cover for a shortage of locomotives, BR Class 08, 08920, is seen working hard with a rake of wagons on 28 September 1983. *(A.J. Booth)*

268. Haunchwood Colliery. GOOD LUCK Hunslet 498 of 1890 shows a much earlier design, complete with lift-up smokebox door.
It is pictured here on 2 March 1963 after transfer from Griff Colliery, where it had worked for the previous 72 years.
(Industrial Railway Society/K.J. Cooper Collection)

269. Haunchwood Colliery. Originally built for use at Coventry, North British 24564 of 1939 stands in front of the screens on 5 March 1967 awaiting transfer to Newdigate. This large locomotive found a ready buyer for preservation, and can be seen today – in full working order, at the Buckinghamshire Railway Centre, Quainton Road.
(Industrial Railway Society/J. Hill Collection)

270. Newdigate Colliery. Another locomotive which spent its entire life at one location is No. 3 Peckett 1586 of 1922, photographed on 30 August 1962. It was eventually cut up for scrap in 1968.
(Industrial Railway Society/K.J. Cooper Collection)

271. Pooley Hall Colliery. KAPAI Peckett 1532 of 1920 stops work for a photograph. The picture is not dated but, judging by the wagons being hauled, it would seem to have been taken shortly after nationalization in the late 1940s.
(Industrial Railway Society – K.J. Cooper Collection)

272. Gibbs & Canning Ltd, Glascote. A view showing No. 2 Kerr Stuart 4226 of 1930 in the sidings with its crew. The locomotive was originally built in 1923, but no buyer was found until seven years later.
(Industrial Railway Society – H.W. Robinson Collection)

273. Nechells Gas Works. A scene which typifies industrial railways, with Peckett 2081 of 1947 busy at work on 17 July 1960. This is another locomotive which survived into preservation, and is now at the Foxfield Light Railway, near Stoke-on-Trent. *(Industrial Railway Society/J. Hill Collection)*

274. Nechells Gas Works. One of the small, high pressure, vertical boilered locomotives built by Sentinel of Shrewsbury – 9617 of 1956, photographed on 28 February 1959. This design did not prove to be too successful, and this locomotive was scrapped in 1968 after just 12 years service. *(Industrial Railway Society)*

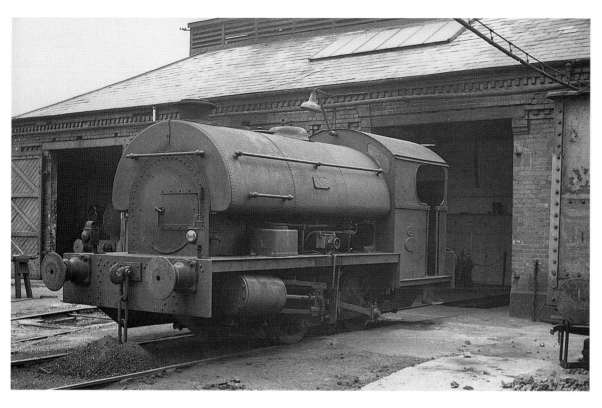

275. Windsor Street Gas Works. Peckett 2058 of 1944 stands outside the shed on 17 July 1960. This was a typical industrial locomotive shed which at one time could be found at most locations around the country.
(Industrial Railway Society/J. Hill Collection)

276. Hams Hall Power Station. Robert Stephenson & Hawthorn 7151 of 1944 working with a train of empty wagons on 22 April 1978. These large locomotives were very powerful, and quite a number of them ended up in preservation; this locomotive can now be seen working on the Avon Valley Railway in Bristol. *(A.J. Booth)*

277. Nechells Power Station. Another of the large Robert Stephenson & Hawthorn locomotives – 7684 of 1951, working on 3 June 1970. This also survived for preservation, and is now on display at the Market Bosworth Light Railway in Leicestershire. *(J.A. Peden)*

278. Nechells Power Station. The replacement for the steam locomotives was this six coupled hydraulic diesel locomotive – Baguley Drewry 3681 of 1972, seen here on 21 September 1976. The power station was closed completely in 1982 and, as no buyer could be found, this modern locomotive was cut up for scrap two years later. *(A.J. Booth)*

279. Austin Motors, Longbridge. ABERNANT Manning Wardle 2015 of 1921 at work on 19 July 1950. This locomotive ended up in a children's playground in Birmingham in 1964, and spent the next 25 years there before being 'rescued'. It is now undergoing restoration at North Woolwich in London.
(Industrial Railway Society – K.J. Cooper Collection)

280. Austin Motors, Longbridge. This was one of the most powerful steam locomotives built for industry, originally used at the Steel Company of Wales's Margam Works. VICTOR Bagnall 2996 of 1950 was photographed in 1963, and can now be seen working trains on the Strathspey Railway in Scotland.
(Industrial Railway Society – K.J. Cooper Collection)

281. Morris Motors, Washwood Heath. PROSPECT Hawthorn Leslie 2479 of 1900, which was kept in immaculate condition, is seen here on 31 May 1950. The locomotive lasted for another ten years before being replaced by a diesel.
(Industrial Railway Society/K.J. Cooper Collection)

282. ICI, Witton. Originally built at Crewe in 1865 for the LNWR (No. 3042), this locomotive was purchased in 1919, and worked regularly until the early 1950s until acquired by the British Transport Commission. It is now on display at the National Railway Museum in York.
(Industrial Railway Society/K.J. Cooper Collection)

283. Bromford Bridge Tube Works, Erdington. Kerr Stuart 3047 of 1918 was the first locomotive to work here, but when this photograph was taken on 14 October 1961 it was very much out of use, and was scrapped a few months later.
(Industrial Railway Society – K.J. Cooper Collection)

284. Bromford Bridge Tube Works, Erdington. This site is adjacent to the M6 Motorway, and is one of the few locations which still uses rail. Sentinel 10098 of 1962 is part of their current locomotive fleet, and is seen here working on 30 September 1986. *(A.J. Booth)*

285. Metropolitan-Cammell, Saltley. ALICE Vulcan Foundry 1451 of 1895 was one of a fleet of elderly locomotives which worked here until the mid-1950s. It is seen in the photograph working in the yard on 7 July 1951.
(Industrial Railway Society – K.J. Cooper Collection)

286. Metropolitan-Cammell, Saltley. Another of the locomotives at this plant was Avonside Engine 1492 which was delivered new in 1905, and despite its age was still in full working order when photographed on 7 July 1951.
(Industrial Railway Society – K.J. Cooper Collection)

287. Cadbury, Bournville. No. 1 Avonside Engine 1977 of 1925, showing the distinctive Cadbury livery carried by all their locomotives, photographed on 4 March 1961. This locomotive is now on display in the Birmingham Railway Museum at Tyseley. *(Industrial Railway Society Collection)*

288. Fort Dunlop, Erdington. The last locomotive to work here was this diminutive diesel built by Motor Rail in 1972 (No. 9932), seen in the photograph on 26 April 1978. After the rail system was closed the locomotive was rebuilt to 2' 0" gauge, and is now working in Wiltshire quarrying stone for use in the restoration of Salisbury Cathedral. *(A.J. Booth)*

289. Minworth Sewage Works. An extensive 2' 0" gauge railway has been in operation here since 1906, and was first operated by steam locomotives. Two of them survived until 1961, and Bagnall 2088 of 1918 was photographed on 4 March 1961 just before being sent away for preservation. It has now been restored to full working order on a private railway in Kent *(J.A. Peden)*

290. Minworth Sewage Works. The rail system survived until 1989 when it was replaced by road transport. Motor Rail 40SD501 of 1975 is seen on 19 August 1983 with a train of empty skips crossing Water Orton Lane en route from the tip to the sludge beds. *(J.A. Peden)*

291. G. Cohen, Kingsbury. A small scrapyard adjacent to the Birmingham to Derby line still operates rail traffic and, when photographed on 9 April 1987, North British 27939 of 1959 was moving scrap wagons to the BR sidings. *(A.J. Booth)*

292. The end of the line. A 40 hp locomotive built by the Motor Rail & Tramcar Co. in use by contractors lifting part of the Hampton-in-Arden to Whitacre line. It is seen near Packington with a demolition train on 9 September 1951.
(F.W. Shuttleworth Collection)

INDEX

'This is THE END!'